SKYBOX PRESS

Foreword	12
Introduction	14
Regular Season	18
NLDS vs. Brewers	44
NLCS vs. Dodgers	60
World Series vs. Astros	80

FOREWORD
Dansby Swanson

As we progressed through the World Series parade and saw all the kids out of school, I was reminded of how big of a deal this really was. The Braves last won the World Series in 1995, when I was one year old. So, growing up in the Atlanta area, I always looked forward to the possibility of the Braves—and the Hawks and the Falcons—winning a world championship.

That never happened, and it's amazing that it took nearly three decades for the city to celebrate another title. But this should give all of us more reason to embrace and savor the thrill of this championship. You can't ever take these things for granted. When the parade ended, we were all joking and saying, "Can we turn around and do that again?"

The energy was so real, and the excitement was special. The city really did itself justice with how the fans came out and cheered us on and honored us. I'll forever be grateful not only that I won a World Series but also that I helped do it for my hometown team.

Because I was so busy playing baseball, basketball, and other sports growing up, I didn't go to a lot of Braves games. But like all the other kids, I rooted for Chipper Jones, Andruw Jones, and everything else related to the Braves. One of my favorite memories was being at Turner Field for a game when Chipper hit two home runs against the Cardinals.

I went away to play college baseball for Vanderbilt University, and then I was selected by Arizona with the first overall pick in the 2015 MLB Draft, but I always thought about coming home. And then, on December 8, 2015, I was having dinner when I found out that the D-backs had traded me to the Braves. I remember going and shooting baskets for a couple hours to try and process how my life had changed and the fact that I was really coming home.

Atlanta is such a unique place. It's had a grasp on me ever since I was a little kid. To be able to share winning a World Series title with the city of Atlanta is amazing. I live and die with the Falcons every Sunday during football season, and I was at the game when the Falcons blew their 28–3 lead to Tom Brady and the Patriots in Super Bowl LI in Houston. So it was extra special to secure our World Series title in Houston.

And with this victory, we flipped the script and showed that Atlanta sports teams can win the big one.

Over the years, I've watched countless replays of Marquis Grissom catching the final out of the 1995 World Series, and so it feels surreal to me to think that decades from now, the highlights from the 2021 World Series will show me fielding the series-ending ground ball and making the throw to Freddie Freeman for the final out.

If you ask me, it's a happy ending to a storybook season.

INTRODUCTION
Brian Snitker

More than a week after winning the World Series, I was still getting congratulatory calls from friends and other managers. Those managers who have won one before have said this will change my life forever. It's still hard to believe. Nothing can ever take this away from us. I still sit in that same recliner where I used to watch everybody else do it, and I still can't believe I continue to live that thrill.

My only regret is that Hank Aaron wasn't alive to see us win that world championship. But I'm quite confident he was looking over us the entire season. Hank was like a second father to me, and I'll always be appreciative of everything he did, including giving me my first coaching job when my days playing for the Braves in the Minor Leagues ended in 1980. I couldn't ask for anything more than to have had Hank's support throughout my 40-plus years within the Braves organization.

At the same time, I couldn't have asked for a better mentor than Bobby Cox. I learned so much just from sitting there watching Bobby do what he did on a daily basis. Being on his coaching staff for the last four years of his managerial career enriched what I had learned as a manager in the Minor Leagues, and it prepared me for the opportunity I received six weeks into the 2016 season, when I became the Braves' manager.

It was a thrill to win the first of our four National League East titles in 2018, and both the 2019 and 2020 seasons were special in their own ways. But what we went through as a team and organization this past year made winning the 2021 World Series even more satisfying. We lost Marcell Ozuna in late May, and then Ronald Acuña Jr. suffered his season-ending right knee injury on July 10. How many teams could bounce back from losing two of its first four hitters? You also have to remember that Mike Soroka had torn his Achilles again, and we were without Travis d'Arnaud for three months because of a thumb injury.

I'll always be appreciative of the way our guys fought and remained focused throughout the year. What our president of baseball operations, Alex Anthopoulos, did at the trade deadline was fabulous. Acquiring Jorge Soler, Eddie Rosario, Joc Pederson, Stephen Vogt, Adam Duvall, and Richard Rodríguez within two weeks after the All-Star break changed everything about our season.

Making this even more special was the fact that I have always been with the Braves—going back to the start of my playing career in the Minor Leagues. This was the club that raised me. Guys like Hank Aaron, Jim Beauchamp, Bobby Cox, Bruce Dal Canton, and Paul Snyder all played a significant role in influencing my career. They also influenced my son, Troy, throughout the years. As one of the Astros' hitting coaches, Troy has been to a World Series two of his first three seasons as a Major League Baseball coach.

Being able to compete against my son in a World Series was special. These kinds of things just don't happen. When Troy returned home to Atlanta after the series, it was a bigger hug than normal. There were just so many things that made the year so special.

And to the fans who've been there for us—this season, through the unprecedented times of the pandemic, and the 26 years since we last won the World Series—this book filled with moments and memories is for you. We couldn't have done it without you.

REGULAR SEASON

Ronald Acuña Jr. admires his 456-foot blast over the center field fence to give the Braves the lead in an 8–1 win over the Phillies in the home opener.

Coming off the COVID-shortened 2020 season that ended with the Braves just one victory shy of a World Series appearance, Atlanta entered 2021 with high hopes, both for continued success on the field and a return to normalcy off it.

Led by reigning National League MVP Freddie Freeman and All-Star Ronald Acuña Jr., the Atlanta offense again had the potential to be one of the game's best. As for the pitching staff, veteran Charlie Morton and young Max Fried were set to anchor a rotation that looked forward to the return of All-Star Mike Soroka from a torn Achilles tendon. But the best-laid plans quickly went awry.

The Braves got swept in Philadelphia to begin the season. Atlanta would lose its first four games, then win the next four, then lose the next four—providing a glimpse of the roller coaster the Braves would ride throughout the season.

Every team endures injuries, but the Braves felt especially snakebit: Travis d'Arnaud tore a left-thumb ligament on May 1, Marcell Ozuna fractured two fingers in late May, and Soroka never returned after tearing his Achilles tendon again in June—and then the big blow came on July 10 when Acuña was lost for the season after suffering a torn right anterior cruciate ligament.

At the All-Star break, the Braves were one game under .500 (44–45) and in third place in the division, 4-1/2 games back of the Mets. President of Baseball Operations Alex Anthopoulos used the time off to begin revamping the roster, acquiring outfielder Joc Pederson, who had been to the playoffs in each of his six full seasons and had won a World Series with the Dodgers in 2020.

The outfield overhaul continued with a trio of trade deadline moves that added Jorge Soler from the Royals, Adam Duvall from the Marlins, and Eddie Rosario from the Indians. The Braves also swung a deal with the Pirates for reliever Richard Rodríguez, who helped solidify the bullpen.

The results were immediate, as Atlanta won 16 of 18 games in the first three weeks of August. An 8–4 home win over the Nationals on August 6 gave the Braves their first winning record of the season, and a road victory in Washington on August 15 put Atlanta atop the NL East, a spot the Braves would not relinquish.

Duvall and Soler added power to a lineup that got MVP-caliber seasons from both Freeman and Austin Riley. Ozzie Albies and Riley both enjoyed their first 30-home run, 100-RBI seasons. Rosario got rolling down the stretch and hit for the cycle on September 19 in San Francisco. Max Fried won four starts and Will Smith notched eight saves in August, and Atlanta stretched the division lead to five games toward the end of the month—but then a four-game skid in mid-September shrunk that lead to just a half-game.

Determined to avoid a Wild Card Game matchup against the resurgent Giants or the reigning-champion Dodgers, the Braves reeled off a 12–2 finish to the regular season, including a three-game home sweep of the Phillies highlighted by home runs from Soler and Riley and Smith's career-best 37th save in the September 30 clincher, as the Braves won a fourth-straight NL East title and a spot in the NLDS.

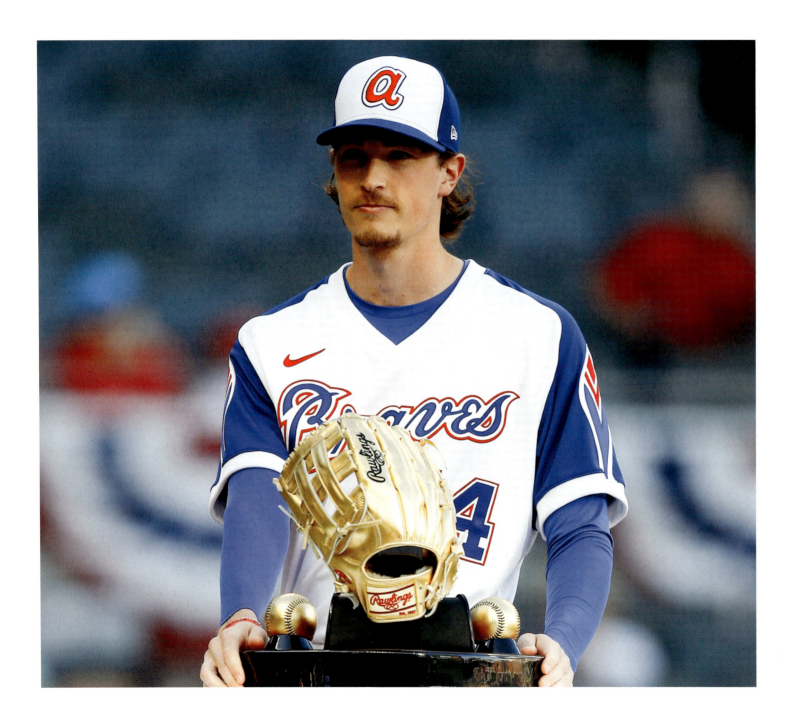

Left
Max Fried becomes the first Braves pitcher since Greg Maddux to receive a Gold Glove.

Opposite
With everyone wearing No. 42 on Jackie Robinson Day, Dansby Swanson soaks in the glory after his walk-off single caps off a comeback win against Miami.

Opposite
Freddie Freeman flashes the leather by reaching far over the dugout railing to snag a foul pop-up against the Diamondbacks.

Top
Ronald Acuña Jr. leaps to the top of the fence to rob Cubs leadoff man Anthony Rizzo of extra bases on the first play of the game on April 29.

Bottom
Trailing by three runs in the 12th inning, catcher William Contreras throws down his bat after drilling a game-tying double against the Phillies on May 8; two plays later, he scored on an Ehire Adrianza single to seal the 8–7 win.

Huascar Ynoa led all Braves starters in ERA (3.02), strikeouts (50), and wins (4) before suffering a broken hand on May 16 in Milwaukee, costing him half a season.

Charlie Morton left Atlanta in 2008 after his rookie season and returned 13 years later to lead the team in strikeouts (216).

Dansby Swanson enjoys a (Panda) bear hug with Pablo Sandoval after hitting one of his career-high 27 home runs. He also set career marks for hits and RBI.

Talented young lefty Tucker Davidson came up and made four starts for the Braves before getting sidelined with a forearm injury.

Left
Ehire Adrianza greets Pablo Sandoval, who had three hits and scored the final run in a 3–1 win at Boston.

Opposite
Southpaw Tyler Matzek was one of Atlanta's most effective relievers, striking out 77 in 63 innings while keeping opponents off the scoreboard in 58 of his 69 appearances.

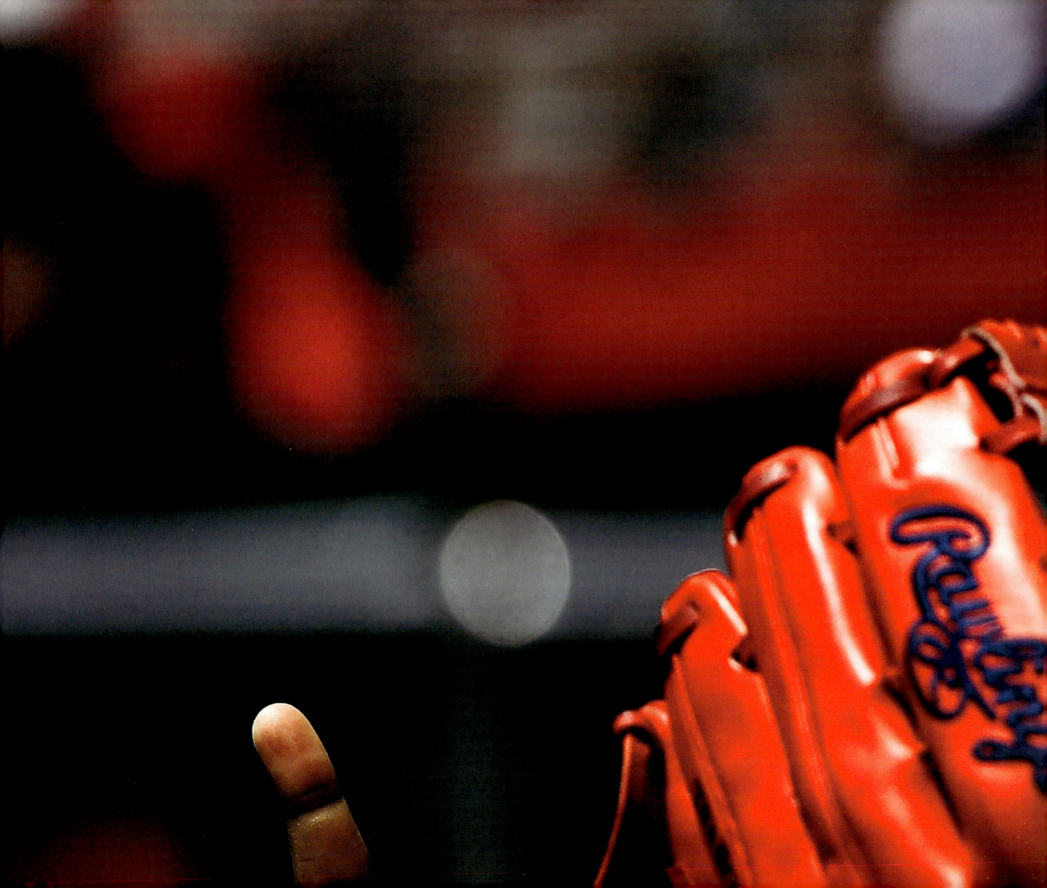

Ronald Acuña Jr. basks in the glow of a strong start to the 2021 season.

Former All-Star and three-time Gold Glove winner Ender Inciarte makes an acrobatic catch against the Reds.

Reigning NL MVP Freddie Freeman drives in one of Atlanta's 20 runs in a romp over the Mets; the 20–2 score was the most lopsided victory for either team in the longtime rivalry.

Top
Pablo Sandoval takes a mighty cut against the Mets.

Bottom
Touki Toussaint bears down en route to a season-best 10 strikeouts against the Phillies on July 25.

Opposite
Outfielder Guillermo Heredia's bat shatters on a pitch by Marlins reliever Zach Pop during a 5–0 Braves win.

A midseason acquisition from Arizona, former All-Star catcher Stephen Vogt, provided veteran depth behind the plate.

Middle-inning specialist Chris Martin's 1.25 walks per 9 innings ranked fifth among all MLB pitchers who threw at least 40 innings in 2021.

Edgar Santana was brought in from the Pirates to deliver mostly late-inning relief.

Ozzie Albies parks an 11th-inning home run for a walk-off win over Cincinnati.

Opposite
Jorge Soler gets high-fives all around after hitting a three-run homer against the Giants.

Right
Closer Richard Rodríguez came over from Pittsburgh and was scoreless in his first nine appearances with the Braves.

Former Cub Joc Pederson smacked a 10th-inning single against the Nats that made him the seventh Braves player of the season to notch a walk-off hit.

Eddie Rosario slid right in with Atlanta after being acquired in a trade with Cleveland.

Top
Austin Riley earned the Silver Slugger Award at third base by leading the Braves with 33 home runs and 107 RBI and leading the league in assists defensively at the hot corner.

Bottom
Atlanta's cornermen and cornerstones, Freddie Freeman and Austin Riley, celebrate the Braves' division title.

Opposite
Who needs champagne? Bullpen mainstays A.J. Minter and Luke Jackson revel in the NL East championship under the cascading waterfall beyond center field at Truist Park.

NLDS 2021

GAME 1	GAME 2	GAME 3	GAME 4
ATL 1	ATL 3	MIL 0	MIL 4
MIL 2	MIL 0	ATL 3	ATL 5

The Braves used to call Milwaukee home, but these fans, getting autographs from reliever Josh Tomlin, are rooting for Atlanta.

Braves vs. Brewers

Having tallied 88 wins in winning their division, the Braves were slight underdogs in the NL Division Series against the Brewers. Milwaukee boasted one of the most feared pitching staffs in baseball, but it was Atlanta's hurlers who took advantage, silencing a Brewers lineup that had faded down the stretch of a 95-win season.

Milwaukee's Cy Young Award candidate, Corbin Burnes, and Atlanta's Charlie Morton waged an epic pitchers' duel in Game 1. Morton limited the Brewers to just two hits before Rowdy Tellez broke a scoreless tie with a decisive two-run home run in the seventh inning. A Joc Pederson pinch-hit homer in the eighth inning wasn't enough to prevent a 2–1 loss in Game 1, nor did it create a hangover, as the Braves turned to Max Fried, who legitimized the MLB-best 1.74 ERA he had produced after the All-Star break.

Fried took the mound in Game 2 and tossed six scoreless innings in Milwaukee. Soler's one-out double in the third was followed by a Freddie Freeman single and an Ozzie Albies double. Suddenly, the Braves had a 2–0 lead over Brandon Woodruff, who would surrender a sixth-inning home run to Austin Riley.

Having split a pair of road games, the Braves came back to Atlanta and claimed a second-straight 3–0 win over the Brewers. Ian Anderson tossed five scoreless innings and Truist Park was introduced to "Joctober" when Pederson drilled a pinch-hit, three-run home run off Adrian Houser in the fifth. Pederson's game-winner put the Braves a win away from reaching the NLCS for a second-straight season. It also further endeared the eccentric outfielder to Atlanta fans, many of whom would come to the park wearing pearl necklaces, a fashion trend Pederson started during the regular season's final week.

With Fried scheduled to pitch Game 5 on regular rest, the Braves gambled by starting Morton on short rest in Game 4. He lasted just 3-1/3 innings, giving up two runs in the top of the fourth, but Atlanta answered with two in the bottom of the inning. Milwaukee scored two more runs off Huascar Ynoa in the top of the fifth, and again, the Braves matched the Brewers with two in the bottom of the fifth. With two outs in the eighth inning, Freeman stepped in against Josh Hader, who had been all but unhittable for lefties during the regular season, and drilled the first pitch out of the ballpark, becoming the first Braves player to hit a go-ahead home run in the eighth inning or later of a postseason clinching game.

Will Smith allowed a leadoff single in the bottom of the ninth inning, but there would be no more drama—or scoring—as Smith set down the final three batters, ending the Brewers' season and sending the Braves to the NLCS for a rematch with the Dodgers.

Top
Pinch hitter Joc Pederson circles the bases after hitting an eighth-inning solo shot for the only Atlanta run in a 2–1 loss to the Brewers in Game 1.

Bottom
Lefty reliever Tyler Matzek appears in all four games for the Braves in the NLDS, allowing three hits and two walks while holding the Brewers scoreless.

Opposite
An owner of World Series rings with the Royals and the Dodgers, speedy Terrance Gore made his Braves debut as a pinch runner for the Braves in Game 2.

Max Fried blanks the Brewers with six strikeouts to earn his first postseason victory.

Jorge Soler gestures toward his teammates after sliding safely into second base with a double.

Freddie Freeman slides home safely as Brewers catcher Manny Piña misses the tag—and the ball.

Austin Riley connects on the second postseason home run of his career.

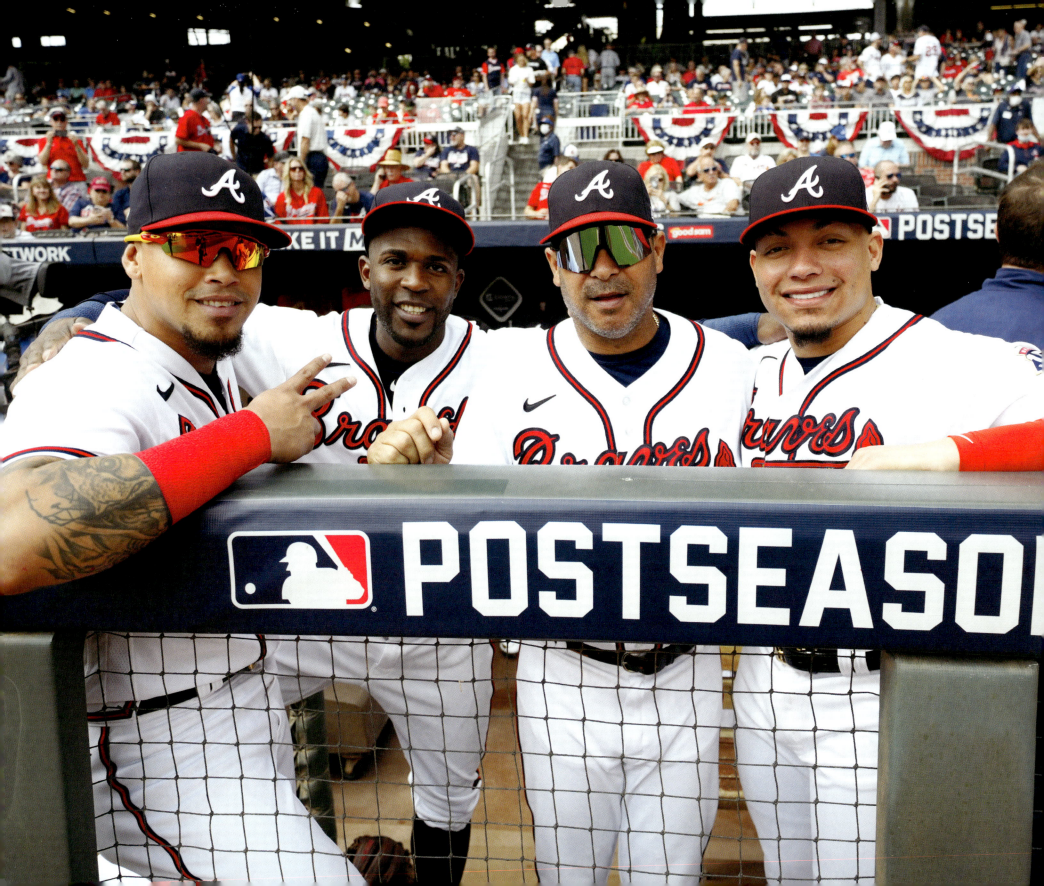

Opposite
Orlando Arcia, Guillermo Heredia, batting practice pitcher Tomás Peréz, and William Contreras pose in the dugout prior to Game 3.

Right
Shortstop Dansby Swanson turns a picture-perfect double play over Milwaukee's Willy Adames.

It's handshakes all around as the Braves take Game 3 to go up 2–1 in the best-of-five series.

Top
Charlie Morton gets the start in Game 4 with the chance for the Braves to clinch.

Bottom
Travis d'Arnaud ties the game at 4–4 with an RBI single in the fifth inning.

Opposite
Closer Will Smith flexes and roars after getting Christian Yelich to strike out to end the series and send the Braves on to the next round.

President of Baseball Operations Alex Anthopoulos, the architect of Atlanta's roster overhaul, embraces first base coach Eric Young Sr.

Freddie Freeman, whose eighth-inning home run put the Braves ahead for good, showers himself in champagne after Atlanta advances to the NLCS for the second year in a row.

GAME 1	GAME 2	GAME 3	GAME 4	GAME 5	GAME 6
LAD 2	LAD 4	ATL 5	ATL 9	ATL 2	LAD 2
ATL 3	ATL 5	LAD 6	LAD 2	LAD 11	ATL 4

Eddie Rosario scores the first run of the series past Dodgers opener Corey Knebel, who threw a wild pitch and then failed to make the tag.

Braves vs. Dodgers

Despite winning 18 fewer regular-season games than the Dodgers, the Braves enjoyed home field advantage in the NLCS because the Dodgers, despite winning 106 regular season games, were relegated to a Wild Card berth after falling short of the 107-win Giants.

Max Fried delivered six strong innings in the series opener, and Austin Riley drilled a home run that tied the game at 4–4 in the fourth. There would be no further scoring until the ninth inning, when Ozzie Albies singled, stole second, and scored on Riley's walk-off single. The victory marked the first time the Braves had won an NLCS game in Atlanta since 1999.

In Game 2, the Dodgers' Corey Seager hit a two-run home run before Braves starter Ian Anderson recorded the first out, but Joc Pederson returned the favor with a two-run homer off Max Scherzer in the fourth inning. LA's Chris Taylor tallied a two-run double off Luke Jackson in the seventh inning, but back came the Braves as Riley's RBI double off Julio Urias capped a game-tying, two-run eighth. With two outs in the bottom of the ninth and Dansby Swanson on second base, Dodgers manager Dave Roberts called on closer Kenley Jansen, who promptly gave up a first-pitch single to Eddie Rosario that scored Swanson for a second consecutive walk-off win.

Because Charlie Morton had started Game 4 of the NLDS on short rest, the Braves opted to hold him until Game 3 of the NLCS. The veteran hurler pitched effectively for five innings, giving up just two runs, courtesy of Mookie Betts' homer in the first inning. Los Angeles ace Walker Buehler had an off night, lasting just 3-2/3 innings and allowing six hits, four runs, and three walks, including a bases-loaded free pass to Eddie Rosario in the four-run fourth inning.

An Adam Duvall RBI single in the fifth inning made the score 5–2, and that's how it stayed until the eighth inning, when Braves reliever Luke Jackson served up a three-run home run to Cody Bellinger that tied the game, and then Betts gave the Dodgers a 6–5 lead with an RBI double off Jesse Chavez. Atlanta fans had to be happy to see Kenley Jansen come out to pitch the ninth inning, but Jansen struck out the side to end it.

Chavez cruised through the first inning as the Game 4 opener, Drew Smyly contributed 10 big outs, and home runs by Rosario, Duvall, and Freddie Freeman helped the Braves build a 5–0 lead through the top of the fifth inning. The Dodgers scratched out a pair of runs to make it 5–2, but A.J. Minter pitched two scoreless innings, and Tyler Matzek pitched a perfect eighth, before Rosario put the game out of reach with a three-run homer in the ninth, and the Braves won, 9–2.

Game 5 started with a bang: Freeman's first-inning two-run home run put Braves fans in a partying mood, but Fried struggled with his

command and got touched up for five earned runs in 4-2/3 innings. Atlanta relievers fared no better, as Chris Taylor belted three home runs and AJ Pollock hit two while the Braves' bats fell silent, as the Dodgers romped, 11–2.

Back home in Truist Park for Game 6, the Braves struck first on an Austin Riley RBI double in the first inning. Los Angeles tied it up on a Cody Bellinger RBI single in the fourth, only to see Buehler surrender a walk, a double, and then an Eddie Rosario three-run shot over the fence down the right field line.

Los Angeles rallied in the seventh inning against Luke Jackson with a double, a walk, and then an RBI double, but Braves manager Brian Snitker squelched that, bringing in Tyler Matzek, who struck out the next three Dodgers and then came back out and pitched a perfect eighth. Will Smith then made quick work of the ninth, and the Braves celebrated their first National League pennant since 1999.

Left
Dansby Swanson tags out Chris Taylor in a rundown, killing a potential Dodgers rally in the top of the ninth inning.

Opposite
Ozzie Albies smiles as he scores the Game 1 game-winner on Austin Riley's walk-off single.

Opposite
Game 2 starter Ian Anderson, just 23 years old, is unfazed by the big stage.

Top
Jesse Chavez sets the side down in the fourth inning; 38 years young, Chavez signed with the Braves as a free agent for 2021—more than a decade after he played with Atlanta in 2010.

Bottom
Reliever Jacob Webb thwarts a Dodgers threat in the sixth inning.

Dansby Swanson and Ozzie Albies are downright giddy after Swanson scores on a second-consecutive walk-off win in Game 2.

Left
Eddie Rosario singles to lead off Game 3, one of 14 hits he belted in 25 at-bats in the NLCS.

Opposite
A.J. Minter aims and fires; his scoreless sixth inning included clutch strikeouts of Cody Bellinger and Albert Pujols.

NL RBI leader Adam Duvall goes back-to-back after Eddie Rosario went yard in the second inning of Game 4.

Drew Smyly deals en route to earning the win and snapping Atlanta's 10-game losing streak in Dodger Stadium.

Former Dodger Joc Pederson's RBI single makes him one of two Braves (along with Brian Jordan) with at least nine RBI through his team's first eight postseason games.

Eddie Rosario can taste victory after hitting his second home run of the game to seal a 9–2 win.

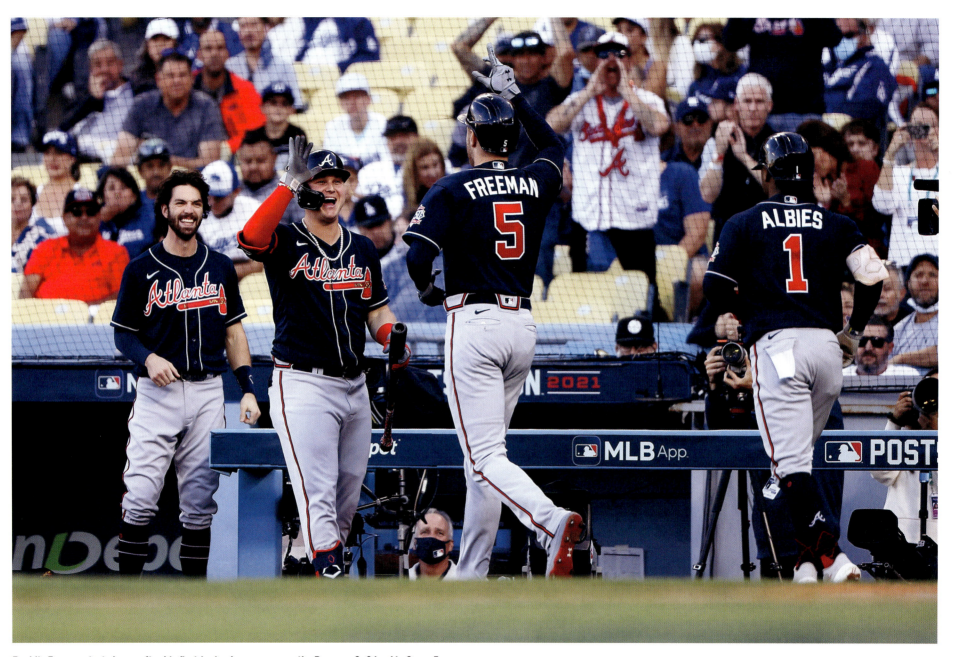

Freddie Freeman trots home after his first-inning home run gave the Braves a 2–0 lead in Game 5.

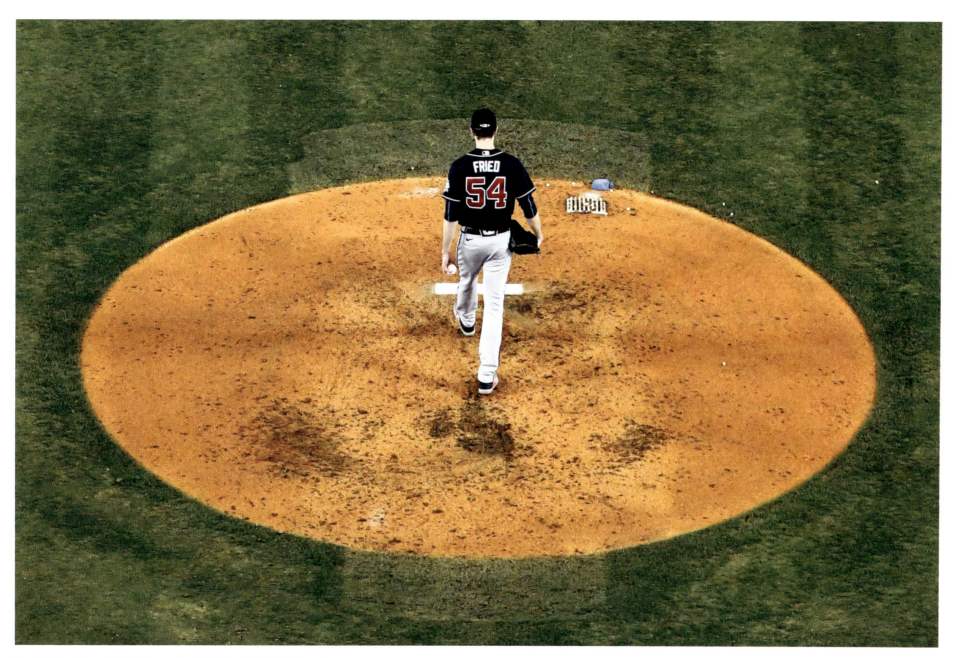

Max Fried was down—but far from out—after taking the loss in Game 5.

Opposite
The Braves score first again as Austin Riley connects for an RBI ground-rule double off Walker Buehler in the first inning of Game 6.

Right
Jorge Soler slides in ahead of the tag for an eighth-inning pinch-hit double.

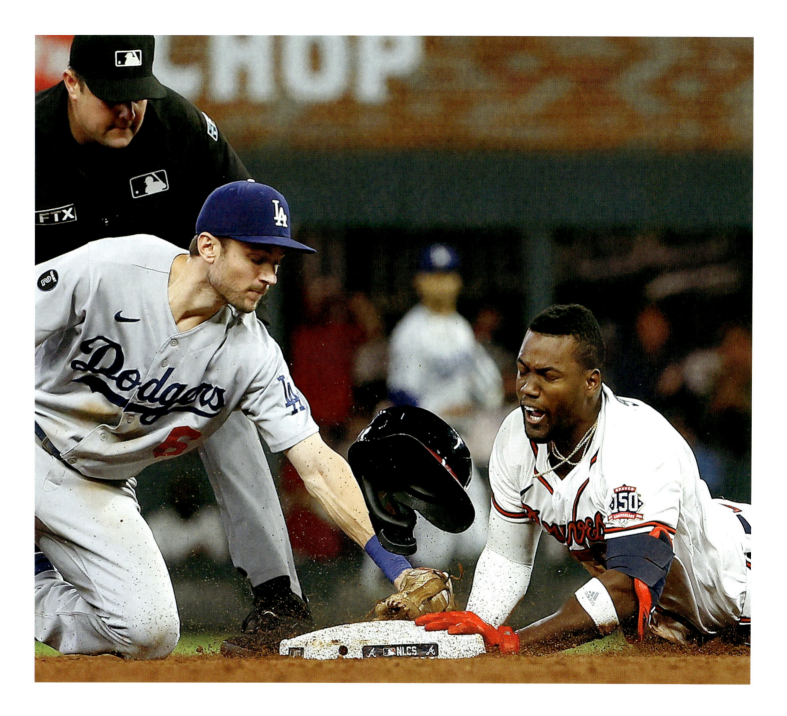

Top
After fielding the final out, Dansby Swanson celebrates winning the National League pennant with Eddie Rosario and Ozzie Albies.

Bottom
Brian Snitker and Freddie Freeman, both career Braves, revel in reaching the World Series.

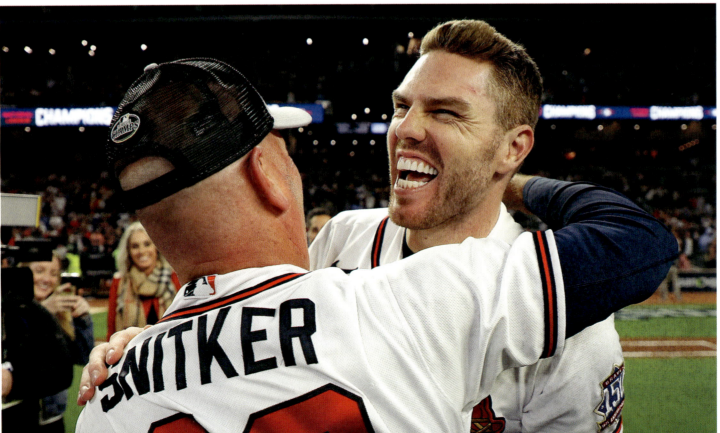

Opposite
Proving the naysayers wrong is sweet, but exacting revenge against the Dodgers and hoisting the trophy before a packed house at home makes this Braves team's achievement all the sweeter.

WORLD SERIES 2021

GAME 1	GAME 2	GAME 3	GAME 4	GAME 5	GAME 6
ATL 6	ATL 2	HOU 0	HOU 2	HOU 9	ATL 7
HOU 2	HOU 7	ATL 2	ATL 3	ATL 5	HOU 0

Brian Snitker and the Braves have their game faces on.

Braves vs. Astros

There were so many storylines surrounding the Braves' first trip to the World Series in more than two decades, though none more compelling than the memory of Hank Aaron. Aaron had passed away in January after having spent nearly his entire career with the Braves. It was Aaron who had given Brian Snitker his first professional coaching job in 1980; more than 40 years later, Snitker was managing the Braves in the World Series opposite some familiar faces in the Houston Astros dugout. Snitker's son, Troy, is a hitting coach for Astros manager Dusty Baker—who was drafted by Atlanta, played eight seasons with the Braves, was mentored by Aaron, and was standing in the on-deck circle when Aaron hit home run number 715.

Jorge Soler looked like Hammerin' Hank when he led off Game 1 with a mammoth homer—the first time in World Series history that the first batter of the first game led off the top of the first inning with a home run.

Atlanta starter Charlie Morton played for the Astros when Houston won the 2017 World Series, but his contribution to this series was cut short after Morton took a comebacker off his right shin to start the second inning; he'd finish that inning and start the third before coming out with what turned out to be a fractured fibula. Morton's determined effort, combined with a strong relief showing by A.J. Minter, Tyler Matzek, Luke Jackson, and Will Smith and at least one hit from every Braves starting position player helped Atlanta claim a 6–2 win.

The Astros bounced back in Game 2, jumping out to a 5–1 lead after two innings and quieting Atlanta's bats. Houston won the game, 7–2, but the bright side for the Braves was being able to rest relievers Minter, Matzek, Jackson, and Smith, who became known as the Night Shift during the postseason.

With the series tied 1–1, the Braves returned home, and Snitker turned to 23-year-old Ian Anderson, who threw five spotless innings. A third-inning RBI double by Austin Riley put Atlanta ahead, and then a Travis d'Arnaud eighth-inning home run added insurance that the Braves would not need, as the Night Shift shut out the Astros. The 2–0 victory was the first World Series game the Braves had won in Atlanta since the Game 6 clincher in the 1995 World Series.

Dylan Lee got the nod for Game 4. Lee had previously made four career appearances, two during this postseason, so he was on a short leash, and Snitker wound up having to pull it after Lee loaded the bases with one out in the top of the first inning. In came Kyle Wright, who set a record in Game 2 for the longest gap (126 days) between a pitcher's last outing and his appearance in a World Series.

Wright induced a groundout, then got a strikeout to get out of the jam and limit the damage to just one run. Wright stepped up and delivered 4-2/3 solid innings of relief, the only other run coming on a Jose Altuve homer. At the plate, Austin Riley halved Houston's lead with an RBI single in the bottom of the sixth, and then the lasting memory of Atlanta's 3–2 victory was

made in the seventh inning: Dansby Swanson's childlike exuberance after hitting a home run to tie the game, followed by the emotional explosion in the Braves dugout when Jorge Soler went back-to-back to take the lead for good.

Game 5 was another bullpen game. Atlanta called on rookie Tucker Davidson, who broke Kyle Wright's days-old record for the longest gap between a pitcher's last outing and his appearance in a World Series; Davidson had not pitched in a big-league game in 138 days. The potential clincher began auspiciously, as Adam Duvall hit just the ninth first-inning grand slam in postseason history, but five Atlanta pitchers could not stop Houston's hitters—including Zack Greinke, who became the first pitcher to record a pinch hit in the World Series since 1923—and the Astros won, 9–5, sending the series back to Houston.

Game 6 effectively ended in the top of the third inning when Jorge Soler launched a monstrous three-run home run that looked to clear the roof of the ballpark as it was still rising. Dansby Swanson and Freddie Freeman also homered, and Max Fried was masterful, pitching six scoreless innings. Tyler Matzek blanked the Astros in the seventh and eighth, and then Will Smith came on and closed out the ninth, getting Yuli Gurriel to bounce a chopper to shortstop. Dansby Swanson watched the ball into his glove then fired it across the diamond to Freedie Freeman—and with that final out, the Braves secured their fourth World Series championship in franchise history, their second in Atlanta.

The playoff team with the fewest regular-season wins won it all, validating every adage, like "That's why they play the games," every cliché, like "It's not over 'til it's over," and every coach who ever preached "There's no I in team," and in the process brought a whole lot of happiness and a little more normalcy to an unforgettable season.

Right
Jorge Soler gets the party started with a mammoth—and historic—home run to lead off Game 1.

Opposite
Following an Ozzie Albies single, Austin Riley keeps the hit parade going with an RBI double to put the Braves up 2–0.

Charlie Morton is helped off the field by head athletic trainer George C. Poulis after taking a comebacker off his leg, which resulted in a fractured fibula that ended his postseason.

A.J. Minter brings the heat; the Texas native replaced Morton and earned the Game 1 win in his longest outing of the season.

Adam Duvall comes up big at the plate (left), smacking a third-inning, two-run home run, and in the field (right), making a running backhanded grab.

Game 2 was a bit of a blur for Max Fried, but the Braves would be rewarded for sticking with their young ace.

Freddie Freemen hustles down the line.

Dylan Lee gives it everything he's got.

Travis d'Arnaud ties the game with a solo shot.

Kyle Wright strikes out the side in the ninth inning.

Top
The first World Series game in Atlanta since 1999 is played in the sixth different ballpark in which the Braves franchise has hosted the Fall Classic.

Bottom
Eddie Rosario receives a hero's welcome when he's introduced prior to Game 3.

Opposite
Ian Anderson dominates, not allowing a hit across five innings.

Opposite
Austin Riley smashes a double down the third base line, sending Eddie Rosario home with the first and only run the Braves would need in the 2–0 win.

Right
Luke Jackson was one of four Braves relievers to hold Houston scoreless and preserve the shutout.

Astros pinch runner Jose Siri steals second base in the top of the eighth inning as Dansby Swanson watches Travis d'Arnaud's errant throw bounce into center field.

Travis d'Arnaud atones for his error in the bottom of the eighth with a solo blast off of Houston's Kendall Graveman.

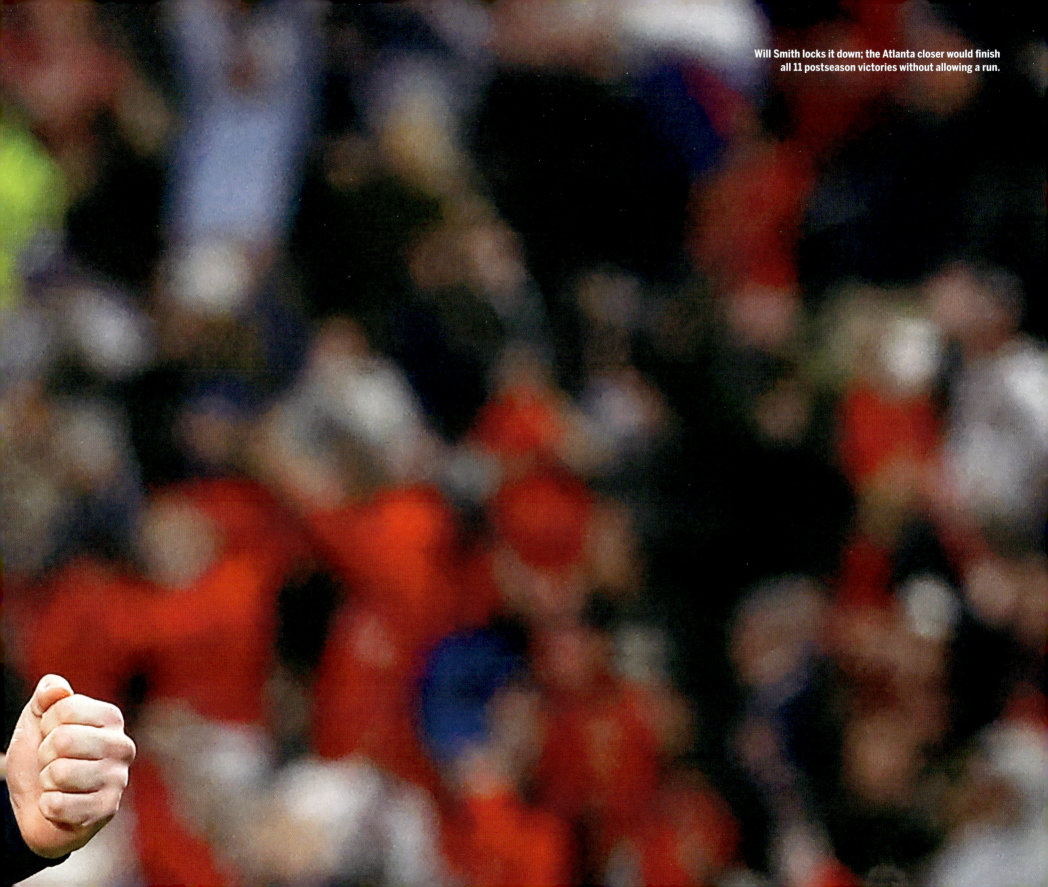

Will Smith locks it down; the Atlanta closer would finish all 11 postseason victories without allowing a run.

Opposite
Game 4 opener Dylan Lee is the first pitcher to make his Major League starting debut in a World Series game.

Top
Brian Snitker makes a quick call to the bullpen, giving the ball to Kyle Wright with one out and the bases loaded in the first inning; Wright worked out of that and limited the damage over 4-2/3 innings.

Bottom
Chris Martin holds Houston in check with an efficient nine-pitch sixth inning.

Opposite
Dansby Swanson ties it up at 2–2 in the seventh inning with a home run off Cristian Javier.

Right
Four pitches later, pinch hitter Jorge Soler takes Cristian Javier deep again, back-to-back, giving the Braves their first lead of Game 4.

Third base coach Ron Washington enjoys the show.

Ozzie Albies and Jose Altuve talk shop at second base during a break in the action.

Opposite
It took a total team effort for the Braves to come from behind and win Game 4, 3–2.

Right
William Contreras, Joc Pederson, and Will Smith enjoy the feeling of taking a commanding 3–1 lead in the series and pushing the Astros to the brink of elimination.

Left
Will Game 5 be a trick or a treat? On Halloween, throngs of Braves fans gather at The Battery for the final game of 2021 at Truist Park.

Opposite
Adam Duvall rounds the bases after becoming just the third player in World Series history to hit a grand slam in the first inning.

Opposite
Eddie Rosario makes a sliding catch on a Yordan Alvarez pop fly.

Right
Drew Smyly pitched in and finished off the final three innings of Game 5.

Houston, you have a problem: Jorge Soler launches a rocket deep over the train tracks in Minute Maid Park, giving the Braves a 3–0 lead in the third inning.

Max Fried comes through when it counts, throwing six scoreless innings, striking out six, and not allowing a runner past first base after the first inning.

Cool-as-ice Tyler Matzek walks off the mound after striking out the side in the bottom of the eighth inning.

Left
Dansby Swanson played lockdown defense all season, so the Braves and their fans had nothing to worry about when the final ball was hit to shortstop.

Opposite
Freddie Freeman, the heart and soul of the team and the longest-tenured Brave, fittingly makes the putout that clinches Atlanta's first World Series championship since 1995.

Opposite
The traditional dogpile on the mound—26 years in the making.

Right
Jorge Soler homered three times in the series and joined Hall of Famers Hank Aaron and Tom Glavine as Braves World Series MVPs.

Left
Eddie Rosario mugs for the cameras as (left to right) Braves CEO Derek Schiller and Chairman Terry McGuirk, MLB Commissioner Rob Manfred, and Fox's Kevin Burkhardt look on.

Opposite
After enduring two unprecedented seasons, baseball fans were treated to an entertaining series.

Opposite
Brian Snitker rejoices with a long-awaited victory champagne bath.

Top
Ronald Acuña Jr. soaks it in; he may have missed the second half of the season and the playoffs due to injury, but he's a key reason the Braves are world champions.

Bottom
Having won a ring with the Dodgers last season, Joc Pederson is the ninth player to win the World Series in back-to-back years with different teams.

World Series MVP Jorge Soler gives a big thumbs up to the hundreds of thousands of fans along the championship parade route.

The spirit of Hank Aaron graced the championship parade, which began at the site of his 715th home run and was attended by his widow, Billye Aaron.

Left
At last, Freddie Freeman gets his hands on the Commissioner's Trophy.

Opposite
An exceptionally colorful team, the 2021 World Champion Braves are appropriately feted with a gloriously colorful celebration.

SKYBOX PRESS

Editor & Publisher
Scott Gummer

Design
Nate Beale/SeeSullivan

Photo Editor
Rebecca Butala How

Writer
Mark Bowman

Captions
David Sabino

Copyeditor
Mark Nichol

Skybox Press wishes to thank Mike McCormick, Jarrett Blass, Josh Brown, James Banks, Matt Meyers, and Gregg Klayman with MLB; Insung Kim, Beth Marshall, and Jonathan Kerber with the Atlanta Braves; Carmin Romanelli, Michael Klein, and Mark Awad with Getty Images; Kyle Hacker, Dan and Harry Goldberg, Chris Molen and Max McGonigle

PHOTOGRAPHY

Getty Images Sport: Dylan Buell, Kevin C. Cox, Mary DeCicco, Nuccio DiNuzzo, Elsa, Adam Glanzman, Sean M. Haffey, Adam Hagy, Quinn Harris, Thearon W. Henderson, Harry How, Todd Kirkland, Mitchell Layton, Bob Levey, Carmen Mandato, Ronald Martinez, Patrick McDermott, Jim McIsaac, Tom Pennington, Denis Poroy, Michael Reaves, Edward M. Pio Roda, Daniel Shirey, Patrick Smith, Casey Sykes, Rob Tringali, Megan Varner, Michael Zarrilli

Icon Sportswire via Getty Images: John Adams, Rich von Biberstein, Cody Glenn, David J. Griffin, Joe Robbins

Copyright © 2021 Skybox Press, LLC.

All rights reserved. No part of this book may be reproduced in any form without written permission from the publisher.

www.skyboxpress.com
info@skyboxpress.com
(707) 537-8700

ISBN: 979-8-9850412-1-7
Printed in the United States of America
10 9 8 7 6 5 4 3 2 1
Published by Skybox Press, LLC.

Official Publication of Major League Baseball. Major League Baseball trademarks and copyrights are used with permission of Major League Baseball Properties, Inc. Visit MLB.com.